MW01608076

SHOTS and SHOOTERS

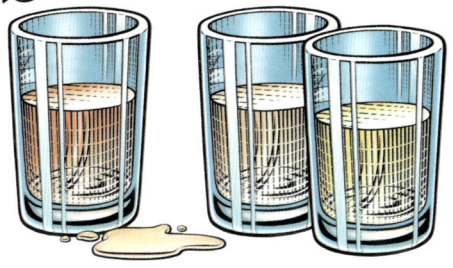

TOP THAT!™

Copyright © 2004 Top That! Publishing plc,
Top That! Publishing,
25031 W. Avenue Stanford,
Suite #60, Valencia, CA 91355
www.topthatpublishing.com

Contents

introduction

Shooters are meant to be fun. The strange names
they are given intrigue and the recipes provide
often unexpected mixes of ingredients.
Drinking them is not like having a quiet beer,
it is an event and something to be remembered—
as long as you don't have too many!

In the bad old days shot
drinking was virtually
confined to a straight
spirit knocked back in
quick time. The first
shooter was probably the
tequila, preceded by a
lick of salt, followed by a
suck on a slice of lime but
now there are thousands
of recipes available.

WARNING
Some of the recipes
here invite you to ignite the drink.
Please be careful when doing this,
particularly if you have long or
facial hair, or indeed both.

Mixology

BASES

Vodka, tequila, and rum provide the base for the majority of shooters.

VODKA

If you want to drink plain shots, vodka is a fine choice. After all, the Russians have been drinking this way for centuries. Nowadays, there are many different varieties of vodka available and even flavored versions can be purchased.

BOURBON

Bourbons can work well as a base for shooters but bear in mind that single-malt whiskies will not. They will burn your throat.

TEQUILA

Tequila is a common ingredient of shooters. A clear, white liquor, it's distilled from the blue agave plant.

RUM

Rum is also a popular shot. There are many different rums available and they come in varying strengths. You should be sensible with the recipes in this book that recommend dark rum as they're definitely not for occasional drinkers.

LIQUEURS

Liqueurs are very fashionable in shooters these days with sambuca being the classic choice.

STRAINING

Most cocktail shakers have an integral strainer. Always use ice cubes when straining, as crushed ice may clog up the strainer.

LAYERING

In layered drinks the ingredients are not mixed as the differing densities allow them to sit on top of one another. To layer a drink, rest the back part of a spoon against the side of the glass. Slowly pour the second ingredient down the side of the glass to ensure it doesn't mix with the ingredient below. Learning the densities of different drinks will help you to layer your own drinks. Obviously the denser ingredient will sit below the less dense.

FLAMING

Flaming should only be done with caution. The stronger the alcohol the more easily it will ignite. One tip is to heat a small amount of the drink in a spoon first. The alcohol will collect at the top, making it easier to light, and this can then be poured over the drink itself.

WARNING
* NEVER add alcohol to an ignited drink
* NEVER leave an ignited drink unattended
* NEVER light it where it might represent a fire hazard, and ensure that no flammable object can come into contact with the flames. Always put the flames out before drinking.

Hairy Lemon

INGREDIENTS

salt

slice of lemon

2 fl. oz/60 ml vodka

MIXING INSTRUCTIONS

1. Rub the salt onto the back of your hand.

2. Bite the lemon.

3. Drink the vodka.

4. Lick the salt.

9

FLAMING
SAMBUCA

MIXING INSTRUCTIONS

1. Pour the sambuca into
a shot glass and light it.
You should see a small,
blue flame.

2. Quickly place your
palm over the glass. This
should put the flame out.

3. Remove your hand
and briefly inhale the
fumes. Shoot.

INGREDIENTS

2 fl. oz/60 ml sambuca

10

Hara-kiri shot

INGREDIENTS

⅔ fl. oz/20 ml ouzo

⅔ fl. oz/20 ml
hot pepper sauce

MIXING INSTRUCTIONS

1. Mix the ingredients in a shot glass then shoot.

2. This is extremely hot so serve with a beer on the side.

Eclipse

MIXING INSTRUCTIONS

1. Pour the grenadine into the shot glass and then carefully layer the rum on top.

2. When the drink has settled, place a cherry in the glass on top of the grenadine. It should float between the grenadine and rum. Shoot.

INGREDIENTS

¾ fl. oz/25 ml grenadine

1 fl. oz/30 ml rum

cherry

B-52

MIXING INSTRUCTIONS

1. Put the coffee liqueur in first, followed by the amaretto and then the Irish cream.

2. When the ingredients have separated into layers, shoot.

INGREDIENTS

⅓ fl. oz/10 ml coffee liqueur

⅓ fl. oz/10 ml amaretto

⅓ fl. oz/10 ml Irish cream

Cerebellum

INGREDIENTS

1 fl. oz/30 ml vodka

¼ fl. oz/7.5 ml
grenadine

¼ fl. oz/7.5 ml
Irish cream

MIXING INSTRUCTIONS

1. Pour in the vodka first.

2. Add the grenadine and
pour in a little Irish cream.
The cream liqueur should
sit in the drink, looking a
little like a brain.

BROKEN
down
golf
cart

INGREDIENTS

½ fl. oz/15 ml
amaretto

½ fl. oz/15 ml
melon liqueur

½ fl. oz/15 ml
cranberry juice

MIXING INSTRUCTIONS

1. Place the amaretto,
melon liqueur, cranberry
juice, and ice in a shaker.

2. Strain into a shot glass
and drink.

21

Eskimo *Joe*

INGREDIENTS

¼ fl. oz/7.5 ml
Irish cream liqueur

¼ fl. oz/7.5 ml green
crème de menthe

¼ fl. oz/7.5 ml
cinnamon schnapps

¼ fl. oz/7.5 ml milk

MIXING INSTRUCTIONS

1. Pour in the crème de menthe.

2. Layer the milk and Irish cream liqueur, and then add the final layer of cinnamon schnapps.

Phlegm

MIXING INSTRUCTIONS

1. Pour the schnapps into a shot glass and layer the Irish cream.

2. Slowly layer the crème de menthe into the glass so that it drips through the Irish cream and the schnapps.

3. Let it sit on your tongue for a second, then shoot.

INGREDIENTS

½ fl. oz/15 ml peach schnapps

drop of Irish cream liqueur

dash of crème de menthe

25

Flaming
GORILLA

INGREDIENTS

⅓ fl. oz/10 ml
peppermint schnapps

⅓ fl. oz/10 ml
coffee liqueur

⅓ fl. oz/10 ml rum

MIXING INSTRUCTIONS

1. Pour the ingredients
into a shot glass in layers,
the schnapps first,
followed by the liqueur
and then the rum.

2. Set light to the drink,
extinguishing after fifteen
seconds, and shoot.

STALACTITE

INGREDIENTS

1⅛ fl. oz/35 ml
sambuca

¼ fl. oz/7.5 ml
Irish cream liqueur

¼ fl. oz/7.5 ml black
raspberry liqueur

MIXING INSTRUCTIONS

1. Pour the sambuca into
a shot glass.

2. Layer the Irish cream
on top.

3. Add the raspberry
liqueur drop by drop
and shoot.

Flame Thrower

INGREDIENTS
¾ fl. oz/25 ml grappa

¾ fl. oz/25 ml bourbon liqueur

1 tsp/5 ml white rum

MIXING INSTRUCTIONS
1. Pour the grappa and bourbon liqueur into the glass.

2. Heat, and then set fire to, the rum in a spoon. Then add it to the glass.

3. Extinguish the flame before serving.

Flaming *Doctor*

MIXING INSTRUCTIONS

1. Pour in the amaretto and then add the dark rum on top.

2. Ignite the shot, allowing it to burn for a short time. Extinguish the flame and shoot.

3. Wash down with a small beer.

INGREDIENTS

⅔ fl. oz/20 ml
amaretto

¼ fl. oz/7.5 ml
dark rum

small glass of beer

33

Bra Buster

INGREDIENTS

½ fl. oz/15 ml vodka

½ fl. oz/15 ml triple sec

1 tsp/5 ml hot
pepper sauce

MIXING INSTRUCTIONS

1. Pour the vodka into the
glass, and then add the
hot pepper sauce.

2. Add the triple sec and
shoot immediately.

Aftermath

INGREDIENTS

⅓ fl. oz/10 ml
raspberry schnapps

⅓ fl. oz/10 ml
grenadine

⅓ fl. oz/10 ml
Irish cream liqueur

MIXING INSTRUCTIONS

1. Mix the schnapps and grenadine.

2. Add the Irish cream liqueur.

3. When the Irish cream liqueur curdles, shoot.

37

Flaming *Russian*

MIXING INSTRUCTIONS

1. Pour the vodka into a shot glass.

2. Carefully layer the rum on top.

3. Set fire to the rum.

4. Extinguish the flame and shoot.

INGREDIENTS

1 fl. oz/30 ml vodka

⅓ fl. oz/10 ml dark rum

Russian *Roulette*

MIXING INSTRUCTIONS

1. Fill two shot glasses with the coffee liqueur and vodka. Place an orange slice on the top of each glass.

2. Pour the sambuca into a wine glass and set fire to it. Pour this onto the shots, allowing them to burn briefly.

3. Put the fire out and shoot the drinks, chasing with a bite of the sambuca-soaked orange slice.

INGREDIENTS
½ fl. oz/15 ml coffee liqueur

½ fl. oz/15 ml vodka

1 fl. oz/30 ml sambuca

2 orange slices

Cream *puff*

INGREDIENTS

⅓ fl. oz/10 ml
coffee liqueur

⅓ fl. oz/10 ml amaretto

⅓ fl. oz/10 ml
Irish cream liqueur

1½ fl. oz/45 ml
whipping cream

MIXING INSTRUCTIONS

1. Put the alcoholic ingredients into a shaker filled with ice. Mix, and strain into a shot glass.

2. Place the shot glass inside a larger glass and fill with whipped cream.

3. Shoot without hands, if you can!

Topless *Nun*

INGREDIENTS

⅔ fl. oz/20 ml peach
schnapps

⅓ fl. oz/10 ml
Irish cream liqueur

drop of sambuca

MIXING INSTRUCTIONS

1. Pour the schnapps
and the Irish cream into
a shot glass.

2. Use a straw to place a
drop of sambuca in the
centre. This will make a
nipple-like dot. Shoot.

45

Mayan
SACRIFICE

MIXING INSTRUCTIONS

1. This is a layered shot so pour in the coffee liqueur first, then the sambuca, then add the tequila.

2. Set fire to the drink. When the flame has gone out, shoot.

INGREDIENTS
⅓ fl. oz/10 ml coffee liqueur

1 fl. oz/30 ml sambuca

dash of tequila

final WORDS

By now, if you've drunk every recommended drink in this book without taking a break you are probably dead. If you've done the same thing with only half of the book you may be lucky enough to be in intensive care having your stomach pumped. However, if you've drunk enough to be mildly merry then you've probably had a very good time indeed.

WARNING
Remember, there is no need to put your life or anyone else's in danger to have a good time. Always act responsibly when drinking.